Pat and Ella were best friends. They'd known each other all their lives. Where one of them went, the other followed. Pat and Ella spent so much time together that people called them the Patella Twins. Right at this moment, the Patella Twins were very worried.

It was Pat and Ella's first day at their new school. Well, it was really Becky McPhee's first day. Where Becky went, so did Pat and Ella. After all, the Patella Twins really didn't have much choice. You see, Pat and Ella were Becky McPhee's knees.

Becky McPhee was a nervous girl. Her doctor said that she suffered from anxiety. Today was going to be a very tough day for Becky. She stood outside the school gates, trying to find the courage to enter.

Pat and Ella had seen the body signs before. Becky's palms were sweaty. Becky's heart was pounding. The lump in Becky McPhee's throat was about the size of Western Australia. Pat and Ella felt the twitch. They both knew what was coming.

'Not again,' said Pat.

'Brace yourself!' said Ella.

And then the two knees began to wobble.
The Patella Twins shook like two lumps of
jelly in a hula hoop contest.

'I can't stop,' said Pat in a shaky voice.

'Relax and calm down,' said Ella.
'Everyone, you know what to do.'

Becky's face scrunched. Becky's fists clenched. Becky's tummy tightened. In fact, every muscle in Becky's body took its turn and squeezed. Then, one at a time, every muscle took its turn to relax. Becky could feel the fear draining from her body. As Becky McPhee calmed down, Pat and Ella finally stopped wobbling. Becky then took a deep breath and slipped inside the school gates.

Becky took a few slow steps and then stopped.

'I can't do this!' cried Pat.

'Yes you can,' said Ella.

'The wobbling makes me feel sick,' said Pat. 'What if it happens again?'

'Remember, one step at a time,' said Ella. 'Surely we're brave enough to at least meet our new teacher.'

'Well, I guess we can manage that,' said Pat.

Becky McPhee took another deep breath and kept walking toward her new classroom.

'What if our new teacher Mr Brown turns out to be a monster?' asked Pat.

'Enough of the bad thoughts,' said Ella. 'Remember, switch on our helpful thinking. Besides, everyone knows that all monsters are green and so Mr Brown can't be a monster can he?'

'Good thinking,' said Pat.

Thinking only helpful thoughts, Becky McPhee arrived at the classroom.

Mr Brown turned out to be a very nice teacher. He greeted Becky with a huge smile. Best of all, he wasn't even a monster. Mr Brown then introduced Becky to her classmates. Even the children in her class seemed nice. Becky took her seat.

The morning went well and before Pat and Ella knew it, the lunchtime bell rang. It was then that the Patella Twins felt the twitch. Pat and Ella knew that the wobbles weren't far away.

'What's wrong?' said Ella.

'Well, what if no one plays with Becky during lunch?' asked Pat.

'Helpful thoughts,' said Ella. 'I'm sure someone will play with her.'

Mr Brown must have been a mind reader. It was then that he asked if someone in the class would take care of Becky during the lunch break. Every child in the class raised their hand. Becky smiled and Pat and Ella felt the twitch fade away.

After the children finished their lunch, everyone took Becky to the oval. They all played soccer and Becky had lots of fun. Pat and Ella got a bit cranky because they were covered in dirt by the end of the game. However, the Patella Twins had to admit that they felt better after all that exercise.

Becky had survived her first lunch hour. Now she knew that it was time to face her toughest test of the day. Pat and Ella felt the twitch as they headed back to the classroom.

When the children entered the classroom, Mr Brown said that it was time for their spelling test. Becky wanted to jump out of her chair and run away. Becky's palms were sweaty. Becky's heart was pounding. The butterflies in Becky's tummy were the size of fruit bats. Pat and Ella felt the twitch.

'I can't do this!' said Pat.

'Be brave,' said Ella.

'What if Becky can't spell any words?' said Pat.

'She practised her spelling last night,' said Ella. 'She can do this.'

Mr Brown called out the first word.

Becky couldn't spell the first word. But she could spell the next one. Becky didn't think about all the words she didn't know – she thought about all the words she did. Pat and Ella felt the twitch fade away. Becky had done her best.

Becky survived her first day at her new school.

'One day down, one to go,' said Ella.

'For this week anyway,' said Pat.

'Small steps,' said Ella.

As Becky left the classroom that day, Mr Brown gave her a high five.

'That's for being brave today Becky,' said Mr Brown. 'You faced up to your fears. See you tomorrow.'

The next day was Friday and it arrived all too quickly. Becky felt sick in the tummy when she woke up. Luckily, Pat and Ella took charge and Becky did her relaxation exercises before she left for school. However, as Becky stood outside the school gates, the signs were back.

Becky's palms were sweaty, but not quite as bad as yesterday. Becky's heart was pounding, but not quite as hard as yesterday. The lump in Becky McPhee's throat was smaller - only about the size of Tasmania. Pat and Ella could hardly feel the twitch. Becky took a deep breath and walked through the school gates.

Becky took a few slow steps and then stopped. All of a sudden, part of her wanted to run away.

'We can do this,' said Pat.

'We sure can,' said Ella.

Becky thought about the promise her parents had made her. Then Becky ran. She ran the last few steps to her classroom.

'Good morning Mr Brown,' said Becky.

Becky's second day at her new school was scary, but not quite as scary as the day before. Pat and Ella only got the wobbles once. Becky tried hard with her reading. She tried hard with her writing. She tried extra hard with her spelling. Best of all, she even made a new friend. Before Becky knew it, the school day had finished.

Becky cracked a smile as she left the school grounds that day. Her parents had promised to take her horse riding on Saturday if she could finish her second day at school. She had done it! Becky loved horse riding. Pat and Ella loved horse riding too.

'Can't wait,' said Pat.

'Me either,' said Ella,

'Speak for yourself,' said Becky's bottom. 'I'm the one who's going to be sore all next week.'

Activities

Describe what Pat and Ella are thinking for each of these images.